Recruiting | Retention

endevis is in the business of talent attraction and engagement...

We successfully attract, motivate and engage talent on all levels, driving organizations in the planning, selecting and developing of great talent through our RPO business solutions.

We find people that will have a dramatic positive impact on our clients' operations.

OUR SOCIAL COMMITMENT

At endevis, we empower a passionate network of people eager to be catalysts in their local communities to share resources and create meaningful change. We support programs that can deliver measurable results for sustainable improvements in the communities in which we serve and operate our business. We invest in organizations that demonstrate a proven track record in addressing key community needs in our areas of giving.

Reviews of Dennis McIntee's Drama Free Teams

In today's health care industry we need our leaders to operate like business owners understanding that service to Patients, Residents and Employees is a priority for our success. Hiring a change management expert who relates well to the needs of this delicate balance was crucial for our people to experience true success and Dennis McIntee was the man for this job.

Mark Ide
CEO, IMG

The heart of this book, for me, is, "There is gold inside of everyone." McIntee calls leaders to be like miners whose focus is on finding the gold. This simple act of focusing on the gold, rather than the dirt in others, will allow us to reduce drama on our teams in meaningful ways. And along the way we may find the gold in ourselves.

Mary Linde
Executive Director,
St. Paul's Towers

You know how drama creeps into your organization and derails your productivity, messes up morale, and eradicates effectiveness? This book solves that problem. Dennis provides a concrete set of steps for creating a culture that is dynamic, effective, and drama-free. And the best part is: he wrote a brief, clear instruction manual... which is the way I like it!

Ray Edwards
Author of *How to Write Copy that Sells*

After spending a decade as an Executive Recruiter, I can tell you first hand that the culture you create determines the success or failure of your business. This book can change your company, change your culture, and change your results. Period. Dennis shows you how behaviors drive results (not policies) and how drama-free teams drive bottom line results.

Jonathan Milligan,
a blogger who helps people

Whether dealing with an employee, your senior leader, family, spouse or friend, Dennis has given us the "CliffsNotes" on how to navigate life Drama-Free!

Donna Kutinsky

Dennis McIntee, the Drama Free Guy, author of Drama Free Teams in Health Care, has taught me more about leading teams and growing my business than just about anyone else I know!

Steve Moran
Senior Housing Forum

I have gone back over my notes from our training multiple times! I have continued to focus on being people oriented daily and the difference has been amazing to me. I got so much out of Dennis McIntee's Drama Free Teams. I am applying Dennis' principles to my professional and personal life.

Kendra Fauth
CMO, CarDon & Associates

While it is true that all business runs on relationships, it is even truer when dealing in the healthcare industry. Whether it is leveraging relationships to motivate clients to healthier behaviors, processing claims, maintaining facilities, or coaching an excellent team to provide services, all phases benefit from Dennis McIntee's Drama Free Teams training.

Chris Krebs
Owner,
Situs Ergonomics

For leaders looking for something to break them out of a stagnant point in their team's growth, this book exposes reasons why your team is not moving, and how you the leader can address that problem. Dennis McIntee cuts to the chase quickly and delivers more than you expected. This book is more than a deal…it is a steal.

Amazon
(Verified Buyer)

I was able to fill three pages of my own "Cliffs Notes" which now contains invaluable direction and practical ways to develop better relationships with teams and subsequently lead much more effectively.

Peter Beaumont

"Trust is like oxygen. You can't see it, but you know when it is not there." Dennis McIntee masterfully uses analogies to clearly communicate his ideas and recommendations. "Mining for Gold", true leaders, they look for the gold in every individual and not at all the "dirt and debris" that surrounds them. I have managed people for over 20 years in a corporate setting and I recommend this book to everyone who manages people.

AJ Slivinski

If your job includes working with people this concise book will make a difference for you. Using just one of the simple techniques outlined in this book will make a positive change to the outcome you are experiencing. This book will pay for itself hundreds of times over.

Nancy
(Amazon Verified)

The gems hidden in this book will help you and your team communicate better and get more done in less time. It's a book you'll return to over and over to make sure you have a "dream team" instead of a "drama team."

Kent Julian

Dennis McIntee's theory, "The culture you create determines the results you produce" couldn't be more true. He gives a step-by-step plan to getting your team to all pull in the same direction and to free you from babysitting duties. It's not creating silly handbooks, but creating ownership and driving motivation - important stuff for any business owner.

Emily Chase Smith

McIntee says, "People rise to the level of expectation." After 22 years in a large healthcare company and 5 years in the public education system, I have witnessed this over and over. Leaders who lead their employees by high expectations, receive high performance. Dennis' book is full of practical wisdom that can be implemented today in any organization.

Hope Schaefer

Dennis hits the nail on the head by detailing the key qualities that must be developed to create a drama-free team. The book is clear and straightforward, providing immediate ideas that can be put into action by any team leader.

Caleb Simonyi-Gindele

This book is different. I came away with numerous insights not just for leading a team, but for realizing my potential in all of my life roles. I hope he writes a sequel for families so many more folks can be helped by his keen knowledge and insight.

Ron Price

This book was a quick read but served up some of the best wisdom on how to manage a team that I've read. McIntee nails the main drama issues around team management. The book is small and extremely practical. As an entrepreneur, this is now required reading for my team right along with "The Go Giver" and QBQ.

R. Steven Kurtion

This book cuts right to the heart of what effective leadership is. Dennis gives practical ideas and steps to begin shaping your leadership…ways to begin changing your thoughts and ACTIONS now! I absolutely recommend this book!

Jodi
(Amazon Verified)

Dennis writes like he speaks; he uses effective analogies and he gets right to the point. There is no fluff in this practical guide to developing and encouraging behaviors that are foundational to a healthy organizational culture. I appreciate Dennis's offering of well-illustrated actionable steps with no added filler.

Be1Eagle
(Amazon Verified)

Dennis McIntee's team of consultants have helped transform leaders, teams and organizational cultures with Cleveland Clinic, Cedar Sinai, Rush Presbyterian, Mt. Sinai, Florida Hospital, Cooper University Hospital, Tenet Health, and 1100 other hospitals and health networks in the US and Canada.

 presents...

Drama Free Teams
in
Health Care

 presents...

Drama Free Teams in Health Care

LESS STRESS. MORE TRUST.
BETTER OUTCOMES FOR EVERYONE

Dennis McIntee
The Drama Free Guy®

DramaFreeBook.com   *DennisMcIntee.com*

Endevis, LLC and Leadership Development Group (Dennis McIntee) have an affiliate relationship for the purpose of distribution of this book, and therefore, both parties, may or may not benefit financially from this affiliate relationship.

For general information about our products or services, please visit our websites or "contact"

endevis.com	dennismcintee.com
Dan Wood	DramaFreeBook.com
VP Business Development	Dennis McIntee
dwood@endevis.com	dennis@leadershipprocess.com
312-415-5637	864-901-7315

Library of Congress Cataloging-in-Publication Data is on file with the publisher.

ISBN: 978-1-73222-450-6 Paperback

978-1-73222-451-3 eBook

978-1-73222-452-0 eBook

Printed in the United States of America

Dedication

The best selling author Robert Schemin once said, "No one ever succeeds alone."
It could not be more true than for this project. *Drama Free Teams in Health Care* is a collaboration with my clients, birthed out of years of practical field work coaching and training teams from a vast array of industries and nations.

To my clients: Thank you. Together we've crafted the solutions and strategies that are helping shape business culture. I couldn't have done it without you.

To Lisa, Andrew, Stephen, Melissa and Joel: I love you all. After 25 years, 25 nations and countless nights being home by yourselves, you've all paid a tremendous price. Your giving and sacrifice has helped birth this book. It's not my book, it's our book.

Contents

Don't Have Time to Read This Book?
www.DramaFreeBook.com
Experience the Entire Book with Videos and
Audio Files, Right Now!

Foreword

"Community unites us, it binds us, empowers us giving us the collective strength to make the world more inclusive."   *—Neil Milliken*

My father always said, "What is the hardest thing to get and the easiest thing to lose…your reputation." Personal and business brands are vitally important, your brand represents what you do…not what you say.

Trust is the foundation of a brand's ability to influence, just as character is the cornerstone of our personal brand. Each interaction we have, every day, with businesses and people is our chance to reinforce trust and demonstrate our character, through our choices and actions. Your brand is your promise, it is your pledge and it is your commitment.

Therefore, our most important resource is our people. People matter. All people. Relationships and collaboration are at the core of all we do, and all we achieve, from the mundane to the spectacular.

Today our healthcare client organizations are working tirelessly to keep their promise of providing clinical excellence with compassionate care for better patient and resident outcomes. Healthcare executives tell us the diversity and complexity of their talent management challenges, especially in engagement and retention, impact every aspect of their care delivery capability.

Attracting, engaging and retaining talent today in Health Care is difficult, rapidly shifting and always evolving. Across the complete spectrum of healthcare delivery, the national job growth forecast is 18% by 2026 (BLS). Meanwhile, Health Care ranks third nationwide in turnover rates (Becker's Hospital Review). Due to the expanding continuum of care, healthcare professionals, clinical and non-clinical, now have more choices in job duties and roles they perform, and more employers from which to choose. Unfortunately, the number of first-year healthcare employees leaving the industry has reached as high as 21% as well.

The health care organizations who are investing in their people every step of the way from talent attraction to engagement and retention to ongoing professional development are winning the race for talent with greater chance to fulfill their mission and deliver on their brand promise.

More and more, our client organizations are asking for additional support, resources and thought leadership in talent attraction, employee engagement and retention. In the service of our client organizations' growing needs we are expanding our RPO business solution capabilities to provide access to research, resources, evidence-based outcomes, training systems and thought leaders.

Dennis McIntee, The Drama Free Guy®, has helped healthcare organizations transform their work culture, increase the health and effectiveness of their leaders and their teams, and effectively navigate change initiatives with lasting impact for hundreds of thousands of healthcare professionals nationwide.

After experiencing Mr. McIntee's training within our endevis community, and witnessing our own people use his Drama Free Team strategies, we were inspired to collaborate with him on *Drama Free Teams in Health Care.* In these challenging, turbulent, and competitive times, we invite you to consider the principles and strategies Dennis provides you here. You may find yourself using some of Mr. McIntee's quotes in your next team meeting, and more importantly, using one of his strategies immediately, just as so many of our people have in our endevis community.

Ron Walters
Senior Managing Partner
endevis Recruiting | Retention
Toledo, Ohio

The Culture You Create Determines the Results You Produce

"Your plan is useless if your team can't execute."

I was raised in Southwest Florida near the home of Tropicana orange juice. I grew up picking the oranges and grapefruit from my grandparents' citrus trees. Still to this day, I love the taste of fresh grapefruit picked from a tree. I enjoyed the warm winters and sunny days. If you've ever visited Sarasota or Fort Myers, you know there is a distinct climate in this area of the country. It has a unique feel. This feeling carries special emotions for me. I'm sure you have a special place in your heart for certain climates.

I've been privileged to live in three different nations and visit over fifty countries. I discovered every area of the world has a unique climate. Some areas I love, like Lucerne, Switzerland, and others were not as enjoyable.

There's one thing I cannot deny: each area of the world carries its own unique flavor. Each area of the world has a certain feel to it because of its blend of weather, language, values, and beliefs. You might not be able to articulate exactly what it is, but you can feel it. Your organization is no different.

Based on your team members' collective beliefs, values, language and vision, your organization has a culture. It might be difficult to describe, but it's the secret ingredient that creates amazing results, or stifles the life energy out of your company.

A friend of mine told me a story about Google. They assert they can predict if an employee will make it with the company according to how "Googly they are." When asked what that means, they can only reply, "We're not sure what it is, but we know it when we see it." Each organization carries its own unique blend of culture.

I often wonder why oranges grow primarily in Florida. Why is it that I do not see fields and fields of orange groves when I'm traveling through northern Minnesota as I do when I'm back home in South Florida? You and I both know it's because there is a different climate in each region. Each climate produces a different product. The weather, soil, and other factors are more conducive to a certain agriculture. It's the climate that determines those results, not the seed. I can take orange seeds and plant them in Minnesota, but the conditions there do not permit the seeds to take root and grow. The same happens in organizations.

You might have the seeds of a great company. You have the right equipment and a great strategy. You may have a fabulous product or service and be in the perfect location. You may have the seeds of greatness in your hands, but if you don't create the right culture, those seeds will not grow.

Earlier this year, I facilitated a two-day strategic planning session with a healthcare company. It was a great two days of debate as the executives sat around the room deciding on what they should focus and where they should allocate resources. Toward the end of the training, I simply asked the question that stopped everyone in their tracks. **"Can each of your facilities execute on this plan?"** Sadly, the answer was no. They had spent two days debating what to do, but didn't give much thought to how they would accomplish their objectives. And Hope is not a Strategy. You've probably heard, "Culture trumps strategy."

Execution trumps strategy, too. I think they had created a great plan, but without a process for execution, that plan was worthless. A great strategy combined with a mediocre culture generates average results, sometimes poor results. But an average strategy with a great culture surprisingly, oftentimes produces better results. What's the secret sauce to success? Culture! It makes or breaks organizations.

To succeed today, you need great strategy. But don't spend all your energy on creating plans without focusing on creating a culture that can execute on those ideas. If you can't execute you can't succeed. You can possess seeds of strategy, but if you don't have climate or culture that can grow that plan, the seed is worthless. **Culture trumps strategy**.

Each year thousands of dollars are spent on developing strategies that accomplish nothing. I know. I'm brought in to facilitate strategic planning sessions. I created *The Leadership Process*™ to help organizations develop their strategy and focus on increasing execution.

At the end of the day, results are the name of the game. Sadly, many leaders believe results are based on strategy. Just because we can write it on a white board doesn't mean we can execute. Strategy and execution are two different things. Strategy is based on ideas, but execution flows from behavior. Many leaders love ideas. They're highly creative and great abstract thinkers. Every organization needs this skill. But it takes more than just an idea to succeed. This is where many companies fall short. They have amazing ideas, but no execution. In the beginning I was guilty of this same thinking. I thought because I wrote it down we could execute on it. I learned quickly there is a big gap between strategy and execution.

This is a book about execution. It's a proven plan that will show you how to increase your coaching skills so you accomplish more with your team. *The Leadership Process*™ is based on over 25 years of research working with large and small companies in both nonprofit and for-profit sectors in over 25 nations.

The principles of creating a drama-free culture that gets results fast are the same, only the application changes. Open your heart and mind.

Though there is a price for creating a high performance culture, I assure you, the prize is worth the price. You can do it!

CASE STUDIES

We invite you to reflect on some of these case studies, as they are each solid examples of Culture trumps strategy and the importance of execution over planning—some show what happens when the organization does nothing and the price they pay for this.

At Leadership Development Group, we have been growing our change management consultancy in senior living, acute care hospitals, community clinics, private medical practices and myriad healthcare niches. We have expert change management consultants who specialize in medical practices, acute care hospitals, independent living, assisted living, hospice and dementia care. One of our consultants has trained and consulted with 9 tribal nations, supporting hospitals, community clinics and Casinos.

With this diversity in experience and expertise amongst our consultants, trainers and speakers, we have worked with hundreds of companies, NGO's and US nonprofits, including licensing our patient satisfaction system to more than 1100 hospitals, and designing and deploying the first comprehensive training system that was customized to the introduction and rollout of

HCAHPS patient experience surveys. We have also redesigned new hire orientation, onboarding and service/patient satisfaction initiatives for a variety of industries, including some of the largest medical practices in the US, including one specialty group in New York with 109 specialty physicians. Interestingly, amongst our consulting team, we have 9 physicians in our extended families—6 physicians in one family! Imagine Thanksgiving meal discussions at their home, when "Obamacare" was first introduced!

Culture trumps Strategy.
Remember, "Your plan is useless if your team can't execute."
These case studies are from acute care hospitals and senior living communities.

CASE #1: "It All Rolls Downhill."

Hospital Environmental Services Technicians (Housekeeping) and Dining Services workers routinely, throughout the US and Canada, bemoan the disempowering and understandably emotionally draining feeling of "I'm invisible in this hospital." The story sounds like this—"Oh our docs treat our nurses horribly, and our nurses, when they are stressed, tend to take their feelings out on clinical aides or non-clinical staff such as engineering, environmental, and dining services departments." This "it rolls down hill" belief sadly, too often, becomes the accepted norm/explanation/excuse for many hospital employees.

Meanwhile, the hospital culture has its own "hierarchy mindset" flourishing with topics such as "Docs wear white lab coats on rounds. But no, OT and PT can't have white lab coats on too!!" And of course, the physician says, "Call me Dr. Jacobs, I didn't go to school for 12 years to be called David here." Yet another perspective to this "I'm invisible" dynamic is the environmental services floor technician (buffing floors) or engineering department tech or journeyman plumber or electrician, who wears his pants with no belt, letting his pants slide down to the point that his waistline of his pants is as low as his hamstrings. Some of these young men speak with their manager about the lack of respect they feel they are having to endure.

Test: We invited 9 EVS floor technicians, at the same urban hospital, to wear belts to work, and to keep their pants pulled up to their proper waistline height. No other changes were made. Over the next few days, EVS floor techs began to share amongst their peers and supervisors, they had met some hospital staff for the first time, some of whom had worked at the hospital for months or even years, yet had never met each other, or at least did not remember meeting one another. These floor techs began to share they did not feel as "invisible" after about 2 weeks of wearing a belt.

Next, we issued white lab coats to all EVS floor technicians, as a test. Within four hours of the start of their work shift, these floor techs were "blown away" at how many people said hello to them while they were wearing white lab coats. The worst part of the test was after we finished the testing, we took the white lab coats away from the technicians. Within 2 or 3 days, we heard many EVS technicians say they felt worse, even more invisible compared to their typical experience before the white lab coats test. However the biggest point was not lost on them, that their attire (properly wearing a belt) had a significant impact in terms of their feeling more respected by hospital staff.

CASE #2: "Pain Management is the Reason"

This example comes from the days of PressGaney patient satisfaction surveys asking the patient to rate how well their pain was managed during their hospital stay. The US government's HCAHPS patient survey initially had a pain management question as well. Today there are physicians who contend some of the current Opioid crisis in America is a result of the over-dispensing of opioids for pain management because of the patient satisfaction surveys in the early 2000's and 2010's. Regardless of the scientific/clinical debate about whether patient satisfaction surveys caused over-prescribing of opioid pain medications, this is an example of how a culture, and a cultural bias or belief can be set within a group of people, even though the scientific evidence has not yet been proven or disproven.

CASE #3: "Eating Our Young"

Nationwide, our consultants hear nursing departments and nursing leaders discussing the "We are eating our young" when referring to how some hospital nursing department or unit nurses are treating their recent RN graduates. We are working to better understand the variety of factors that cause today's nurses who are in their late 40's or 50's to be experiencing burn out, emotional exhaustion and the disheartening experience captured when these veteran nurses sadly or angrily express "This is not the Health Care I went to Nursing school for, all those many years ago."

With the resurgence of expensive Agency nursing solutions for staff shortages in Nursing, and the continued increase in the nursing staff shortage, this issue will linger and will contribute to the "culture" of nursing as a career, for many years to come. Two recent studies predict that by 2024, there will be an 18% increase in the number of healthcare jobs needing to be filled, simply to keep up with the growth demand of health care as the continuum of care continues to expand. These same studies list healthcare/nursing jobs ranking 3rd overall in terms of having the greatest shortage of qualified professionals.

Nursing leaders who have successfully addressed this employee engagement concern along with the generational differences amongst their nursing teams, will be far better off than some of their contemporaries moving forward. The same can be said for approximately 2400 hospitals who have seriously focused on the training of physicians in terms of emotional intelligence, leadership skills, and interpersonal relations skills. These hospitals often continue to thrive with average or even above average patient satisfaction and employee satisfaction, as a result of investing in physician training.

CASE #4: "Can You Reach Everything at Your Bedside?"

Nurses never went to nursing school so they could spend their day running from patient room to patient room, responding to call lights, to discover the patient only needed their crossword puzzle from the windowsill because their last hospital visitor moved the puzzle book there. Hence, hospital leaders who have successfully, consistently deployed the best practice of every hospital employee (clinical or non-clinical) who is in the patient's room, to ask the patient, prior to the employee exiting the room, "Before I go, can you reach everything at your bedside?" Reportedly, this one strategy lowered the number of nursing call lights for patients' non-clinical requests by 18%

to 44%. With this exceptional level of consistent execution over time, this is how you overcome your hospital's inherent "culture trumps strategy" challenge.

CASE #5: "Pain of Change"

Oftentimes in the competitive world of contract management (outsourcing—e.g., Aramark, Sodexo, Compass) in housekeeping, engineering and dining services for hospitals, hospital administrators will want to change outsourcing companies or will want to outsource their in-house management of these departments. However, the pain of change (converting companies, payroll, HR systems, etc.) is sometimes perceived to be so painful, the hospital administration decided not to change contract management companies, even though they were significantly dissatisfied with their current company or in-house management situation. Culture trumps strategy!

Reflection & Action

Culture/Execution trumps Strategy. "Can each of your facilities execute on this plan?" Sadly, the answer was no. They had spent two days debating what to do, but didn't give much thought to how they would accomplish their objectives.

1. List some of the current conditions, status quo ways of doing things, or other challenges/opportunities you are struggling with that are still the way they are, because "Culture trumps strategy."

2. Now pick the one most important/valuable AND urgent issue that you know you should begin to address.

Challenge/Opportunity: _____

In order to finally begin to improve this situation, answer the following:

I need to STOP doing:

I need to START doing:

I need to CONTINUE doing:

Chapter 1

Stop Creating Handbooks

"Policies do not produce results; behavior produces results."

"If we just had a new handbook, this wouldn't be a problem," Phil complained to me when I first began working with his organization. He was a supervisor and couldn't seem to get his direct reports to respond to company initiatives. He was desperately looking for a new policy that would correct his problems. He thought if he could establish new rules, people would automatically obey.

He had just returned from a management retreat where the senior team mapped out the initiatives for the next quarter. After the planning session, he was energized to share the ideas with his team but soon he hit reality. His team wouldn't get on board. "We've never done that," or "It won't work," seemed to be their mantras. He wanted them to be on the same page but it seemed they weren't even in the same book.

Since he only had a plan but no buy-in with his team, there was constant complaining and blaming. Between people bickering about how unfair their job was and the constant gossip that seemed rampant throughout the organization, Phil didn't know how much more he could take.

Phil didn't start out this way. He had taken management courses that taught him the policies and procedures of his job. He had visions of building a staff that was focused on serving customers. He longed to have a staff with trusting relationships that achieved amazing results and had fun in the process. It wasn't turning out the way he hoped and if he didn't do something quickly, this ship was going to sink fast.

My first coaching session with Phil wasn't as pleasant as he had hoped. I opened our meeting together with this, **"Policies don't produce results, behavior does."** It wasn't what he wanted to hear. He wanted a golden key that would solve all his management issues and he wanted me to give it to him in five minutes. There is no one single key that produces results. To believe otherwise is simply naive.

When challenges like this pop up in a team, the initial reaction is to send people through a course. "We need a team building event," some exclaim. Others want to do a ropes course or a motivational seminar. We attend these events and believe everything will be fixed magically. The problem is, after a week, everything goes right back to how it was previously. People do not change at an event. To change behavior, you must have a process.

As a coaching expert I know there are certain constraints to leadership training. If you look at leadership training as only an event, it will not make a difference. If there is no process on the back-end of an event you're guaranteed you won't see changes in behavior. Lasting change requires a plan and a process. The power is in your process, not the event.

You won't have power over any area of your life that lacks a process. For years, I couldn't seem to lose weight. I had poor behaviors with nutrition and exercise. Those poor behaviors were creating my results. It wasn't until I initiated a process for exercise and diet that I began to see different results. It was the process that changed me, not the nutrition seminar I attended. I received great information at the seminar. That's what workshops and seminars give you: Information. But I needed more than that. I needed a step-by-step daily action plan I could follow. After the workshop I knew what to do. But it was the actual daily plan that gave me the energy to carry it through. **To grow and develop any area of your life, you need a process. Your power is in your plan.** Another roadblock to effective leadership training is a lack of accountability. Think about the best leadership book you've read. If it's "really good," you might underline some passages or share them with a friend. But after you've finished the book it goes back on the bookshelf never to be opened again. I call this your "shrine of knowledge." But if you took one principle from that book and built an action plan to use that principle and had a friend hold you accountable for that idea, would leadership improve? Most likely, yes! Many times, it takes accountability to fuel change.

Leadership training that only teaches techniques without delving into the emotions of leadership is also doomed to fail. I know some think emotions don't belong in the workplace because business is simply people doing transactions. However, people bring the whole person to the work place. They bring their thoughts, feelings, values and beliefs. I'm sure you thought you were just hiring a recruit for their skill set, but each team member brings so much more. **Emotion is the fuel of motion. As a leader you have to navigate through people's emotions to change behavior**.

Training and coaching your team requires a process, accountability, and an elevated level of emotional intelligence. As a leader, you are in the people business. Our job is to get results through people. It's a messy job because people bring the whole person, their personal values and beliefs, to work.

To achieve your results, you must change behavior. You have two ways to achieve this. **Nothing ever changes until behavior changes**. You could force compliance by becoming demanding and scaring people into submission**. Instead** of using good coaching techniques that engage people's hearts, **you go after their hands**. This idea forces you to be consumed only with what the person does on the job. This school of thought espouses that you're paying someone for a certain job and you can force them to comply. Leaders who take this route tend to scream and yell at their team in order to create a fear-filled environment where people are afraid of losing their jobs. The problem with this style is people never give their best. They comply out of fear of loss.

The Leadership Process™ adopts the philosophy, **"If you can engage a person's heart first, their hands will automatically follow."** If you help people meet their own core needs in a healthy way, healthy behavior will occur, and amazing results will follow. **Behavior follows beliefs.** Developing great coaching skills that change belief ensures lasting behavioral change.

Reflection & Action

"Policies don't produce results, behavior does."

"People don't argue with their own data."

A leader's job is to take their people on a journey of discovery, by asking more questions, not just telling them what to do.

To grow and develop any area of your life, you need a process. Your power is in your plan. Emotion is the fuel of motion.
As a leader you have to navigate through people's emotions to change behavior.

1. Take a moment to jot down what policies you may be enforcing or implementing, yet now realize you need to shift your focus to the behaviors you want to see.

2. Make a list of behaviors based on this prompt—
If my team would just do _____
then(XYZ) _____ would be so
much better for our (customers, coworkers).

Chapter 2
You Can't Change
What You Don't See

"Feedback is the fuel to changing behavior."

"Dennis, I like truth. Just tell me the truth." Honestly, I thought that was an odd statement from Tom. I'd been working with him for some time now and thought I had always been truthful with him. But the results were not happening fast enough for either of us. I knew if I wanted a different result I was going to have to use a different behavior. So, I tried a different approach. I realized I needed to be more straightforward with him. I needed fewer words with more intensity.

"Tom, here's the core of the issue: You're so direct with people you hurt their feelings. They feel like you don't respect or recognize them and so they back away and don't bring their best ideas to the table." This conversation did not go over how I hoped. I quickly realized Tom didn't like the truth as much as he said he did. He immediately defended and justified his position. Our conversation quickly turned into an argument that neither of us could win.

I learned that day, though people might say they like the truth, many times it will offend them before it helps them. At times the truth is hard for people to hear. Some individuals want people's approval; so, it's difficult for them to separate who they are from what they do. Others fear being wrong so they justify their reasons for why they are, or why they behave, in a certain way. Although it can be difficult to hear, feedback is the best gift.

When you think of feedback as a gift, it changes how you receive it. Everyone likes to receive a gift. But if you don't see feedback as a gift, your first reaction is to reject it. You always receive things how you perceive them. If you grew up in a culture where feedback was discouraged, where the goal was harmony, not honesty, you probably were taught feedback was bad. "Just ignore the issue," you were told. If you pretend it isn't there, then it isn't. This view taints how you receive feedback.

If you can see it as a gift, you will treat it as a gift. What do you do with a gift? First, you thank the person for the gift. I do this because I will always get more of what I'm thankful for. **Through thankfulness you can create an environment that invites more feedback. If feedback is the fuel for me to change, I need all I can get.**

The next thing you do with the gift is unwrap it. The feedback might not be totally accurate, but there is always a measure of truth hidden inside. **Your assignment is to find the truth and apply it.** If you choose to justify and defend your position, you've wasted that gift. Don't discard the message because of the messenger. I know sometimes, feedback is not always given correctly; but, learn to separate the essence from the form.

Several years back I was working with Lance Wallnau. We had finished a training session together in Boston and we were walking into a restaurant. I asked him, "Lance what's my biggest constraint?"

He replied, "Oh Dennis, you're addicted to change. You go from thing to thing and never keep at anything. You jump from this to that and never build a process behind you so you don't keep what you have. Everything flows right through your fingers."

Then Lance walked into the restaurant. I couldn't go in. I stood in the parking lot and cried. It was a hard truth for me to hear, but it was accurate. **That truth set me free**. Ever since then I have become obsessed with building processes behind events and I have seen an amazing impact in people's lives because of that feedback.

In my workshops, I often ask people, "What's the one thing people need the most, but get the least?" There are multiple answers when spring up, but **I believe the greatest gift anyone can get is constructive feedback on their own behavior**. Everyone has blind spots. A blind spot is the thing everyone sees about us, but we don't see. We're blind to it.

Awareness is your first step to changing behavior. You cannot change what you do not see.

If you don't see it's a problem, you'll never reach for a solution. There are times in my coaching this I realize I can't help that particular person. If they don't believe they have a problem, they will never reach for a solution.

My health only began to change when I became aware. In a period of only eighteen months I had put on an extra 75 pounds. I knew I was buying bigger clothes, but truthfully, I didn't see it as a problem until one morning in Dallas. I remember getting out of the shower, and actually taking a hard look at myself in the mirror. I didn't justify it like I had in the past by saying, "I might be a little heavy but I'm not as bad as so-and-so." **I was honest with myself.** I realized I wasn't a little overweight or chubby. I was fat. In fact, I was fat as Texas! It was this day that my health began to change. I saw something different.

Our job as leaders is to help our team members see things differently. It's feedback that helps people think differently. **Our lives are always moving in the direction of our most dominant thoughts.** If we can help people change how they think, they will change how they behave. And we'll enjoy a change in results.

Feedback helps people observe their own behavior. **No one can read the label when they're inside the bottle, so it's our job as leaders to help people observe their own behavior**. When they see and own it, they will begin to change it. Using *The Leadership Process Feedback Formula*™

helps people observe and own their behavior. It's the first step to behavioral change.

The Leadership Process Feedback Formula™

"When (action or behavior) happens, how do you think you show up?"

Using this question invites people to think logically about their actions. Because most behavior stems from emotion, many are unaware of what their behavior is producing. They are simply blind to it. They are inside the bottle. Using this formula, they can read the label and get out of the bottle. Our job as leaders is to help people see behavior so they change it.

"When you gossip about other people, how do you think you show up?"

"When you show up late for a meeting, how do you think you show up?"

"When you forget about an appointment, how do you think you show up?"

"When you are being negative and critical, how do you think you show up?"

"When you fail to follow through on a commitment, and fail to finish on time, how do you think you show up?"

"When you keep talking, and interrupting the other person, how do you think you show up?"

Reflection & Action

Through thankfulness you can create an environment that invites more feedback. If feedback is the fuel for me to change, I need all I can get.

I believe the greatest gift anyone can receive is constructive feedback on their own behavior.

Awareness is your first step to changing behavior.

Feedback helps people observe their own behavior. No one can read the label when they're inside the bottle, so it's our job as leaders to help people observe their own behavior.

The Leadership Process Feedback Formula™

"When (action or behavior) happened, how do you think you showed up?"

1. Look at the examples of "...how do you think you show up?" questions on the previous page. Take time now to identify 1-3 opportunities for improvement you have. (Perhaps, ask yourself, "What do I need to STOP doing, START doing and CONTINUE doing?"). Or who could you ask for constructive feedback? Remember, your only response to them after they give you the feedback is, "Thank you for the feedback."

2. Take one item at a time.

"When _____ happened, how do you think you showed up?"

I showed up _____
_____
_____
_____

What did that produce? _____
_____
_____
_____

What results did it produce? _____
_____
_____
_____

Chapter 3
To Create Ownership, First Give Ownership

People become who you believe them to be!

"You can't teach stupid!" Janice exclaimed to me.

I had walked into her facility to hold a workshop on creating an ownership mentality within her team. At the time, Janice had been an administrator for over 20 years. She had certain beliefs about her team that were holding them back. **What she believed about her team was determining her behavior toward them; and it had damaging results.**

She believed her team was stupid and lazy, so she made rules and policies that made no sense. She required submission and used her title to demand respect. Instead of collaborating on goals together, she created everyone's goals for them. After all, who knew better than Janice what her team needed? She demanded accountability and forced compliance instead of giving ownership.

What was the end result? Employees left as quickly as they could. And to make matters worse, word spread out into the community. They couldn't attract nor keep great people.

Janice didn't seem to understand that people usually don't leave a company; they leave their relationship with their immediate supervisor. She only had a compliance mindset, not a leadership mindset. The more she demanded compliance to the regulations without creating buy-in with her team, the further they distanced themselves from her. She was not getting good results.

Drama-free leaders trust in adult behavior. They assume one basic human need is to be productive. **Employees' behavior becomes a reflection of a leader's belief in them**. Behavior flows from belief. What you truly believe about your team determines how you treat them. How you deal with them determines the results they produce. Your personal leadership beliefs define the results your team produces.

If you assume your people need supervision and specific direction, your assumption could be what's increasing the drama. The lens through which you see your team, will affect your behavior toward them; and your actions toward your team members drive the results you see.

People have a way of rising to the grand expectations we set for them. We all want to live up to people's expectations of us. If we treat someone like they're in a daycare, they likely will sink to those worst expectations of them. If we believe that they are lazy and stupid that's how we treat them; and in turn, that's the behavior we receive. It's a vicious cycle that can be hard to break. In truth, most people are not lazy or stupid, but managers can make them that way.

How you lead determines how people follow. You can apply this not only in your business, but also, in your family, as well. To give you some background, I grew up in a family that practiced the principle, "He who yells the loudest, wins the argument." Because I was raised this way, I took this practice into my parenting. I tended to yell and scream to try and force compliance from my children. Does this, perhaps, describe you? If so, take heart. If I can change, you can too.

One day, I needed my youngest son, Joel, to clean his room. When I walked into our family room he was focused on his video game. In times past, I just commanded that he clean his room, with no regard to what he was currently engaged in. I was a commanding and demanding leader.

It looked something like this: I commanded him to clean his room and he wouldn't listen. I raised my voice a little louder and commanded again. He still ignored me. This went on sometimes for 10 minutes or so, with each command becoming progressively louder, until I stomped my foot and screamed for him to go clean his room. It wasn't until I screamed that he obeyed. I had to sit back and ask myself who was the crazy person in this scenario. I think it was me! I had trained Joel I wasn't serious about what I wanted until I screamed. He knew earlier requests really meant nothing.

I changed my approach, and I saw immediate results. First, I began by getting Joel's attention. I asked him to put his game on pause and look at me. I told him to get ready because in five minutes I was going to ask him to clean his room. I first got his attention and laid out the game plan. After my expectations were clear, I simply gave the request. No yelling or screaming. No demanding or commanding. I didn't have to ask 10 times, I simply asked once. At this point, Joel had a choice. He could obey or disobey. The choice was his.

As leaders, we must make sure we have the attention of our team. Our expectations should be clearly laid out before them. **I've discovered most mediocre performance is due to unclear expectations.** How many times has someone said to you, "Oh, you meant that?" **Clarifying expectations is the leader's responsibility.**

Drama can occur in your team if they feel like they have no choice. When you feel disempowered it's very easy to become a victim and blame others. For many, victim behavior is their modus operandi. They feel like they have no choice, so they play the victim. Empowering your team with choices helps remove the drama. I gave my son, Joel, the power of choice and he responded with different behavior. I treated him as an adult, not a child and he responded with adult behavior.

Seeing your team as adults allows you to have adult-to-adult conversations, instead of adult-to-child conversations. I see this occur in many organizations. People act like children when they wait to be told what to do. Children come with problems not solutions. They deflect responsibility and blame others for their circumstances. They aren't victors looking for a way to make things work. They are victims looking for an outside circumstance to blame. "It's not my fault" is a key mantra. To change the behavior, you must begin to change the conversation.

Ownership is the most powerful motivator in business. It's the organizations that create a culture of ownership that become the most successful. When people feel like they have a stake in the outcome of the company, they take initiative. If they believe what they do really matters, they carry responsibility, make decisions, and solve problems. Owners require leadership, not adult supervision. Many management courses today don't teach leadership. They teach how to run an adult day care.

Giving ownership requires you to see your team as responsible adults that are able to solve their own problems. Your job is simply to help them become successful in their position. Adopting an ownership mentality assumes people are smart, motivated, and want to be challenged regularly to raise their game to the next level. The more ownership you give, the more responsibility they will assume. **The more responsibility they take, the less drama you'll have in your team. When you eliminate the drama, your positive results skyrocket.**

Reflection & Action

People don't argue with their own data.

A leader's job is to take their people on a journey of discovery, by asking more questions, not just telling them what to do.

Employees' behavior becomes a reflection of a leader's belief in them.

I changed my approach, and I saw immediate results.

I will never own my results until I have owned my decisions/choices.

The more responsibility they take, the less drama you'll have in your team.

When you eliminate the drama, your positive results skyrocket.

1. **PAUSE:** Are there members of your team who you "gave up on" a long time ago, or you know you haven't invested your time and energy into the relationship?

2. What specifically can you do this week to adjust your thinking and your approach toward this person? What is the value/benefit to you when you do?

Chapter 4
People Buy Your Why Before They are Sold on Your How

The quickest path to trust is through the door of transparency.

"What do you think Fred really meant?"

This was a frustrating question because we had just finished an excruciating four-hour meeting where we painstakingly went through even the tiniest details of the plan and the process to reach our goals. This meeting wore me out. I felt like this was "death by meeting," and I needed a vacation. I assumed everyone was clear on the goals and we were on the same page.

However, 30 minutes after the meeting, Michelle came to me with her question, "What do you think Fred really meant when he said we needed to produce quicker results in our lab?"

I think this statement had hurt her feelings, but she didn't have the interpersonal skills to navigate a conversation in the meeting. Unfortunately, she went through the back channel by asking me. We proceeded to burn time and money trying to decipher Fred's meaning.

It's a common occurrence in many organizations. We misread intentions and spend countless work hours trying to figure out what someone really meant. Instead of going to the source, team members talk amongst themselves. Unfortunately, they usually come up with the wrong conclusions. Nothing destroys a team's productivity more than misreading intentions. **Misreading intentions is simply a symptom of a much greater problem.**

When trust is low, intentions are misunderstood. In the words of bestselling author, Stephen R. Covey, with low trust, the speed of business slows down and costs increase. I can trace most problems in business to a low trust level. It's the hidden factor that affects everything else. When there is no trust, there is no collaboration. Ideas stop, and territory wars begin. Low trust costs organizations millions of dollars each year.

Trust is like oxygen. You can't see it, but you know it when it's not there. Likewise, if you see symptoms of low trust, it's hard to pinpoint the disease. Without trust, team members shy away from hard conversations. The primary goal becomes harmony. We all attempt to simply get along. We don't discuss the hidden elephants in the room. They may stir up controversy, so we avoid those topics.

From years of working with healthcare companies, I've learned a few things about oxygen. When oxygen deprivation begins to occur, people start to hallucinate. I see this among teams. When trust is low, people also begin to hallucinate. They assume intentions and hidden meanings that aren't even there. They misread the leader's heart and the drama begins. When you see this in your organization, the real culprit is low trust.

Instead of broaching controversial topics, they turn to the gossip channel to make changes. When this happens, your culture becomes a soap opera. In a soap opera, the drama never ends. It goes on and on and on. When you see this, the reason is low trust.

A passion of mine is long-distance running. I've discovered if I want to run faster and longer, oxygen plays an important part of that dynamic. To increase my time and speed, I must increase my lung capacity and pump more oxygen through my system.

Your team works the same way. To produce faster results, your job is to continually pump more trust into your team. **The greater the capacity to trust, the greater the capacity to execute. This is why you need a process for continually increasing trust.**

One measurement of trust is the willingness to have hard discussions and disagreements. Without trust, these conversations become personal. The measuring stick of trust is conflict.

Think about your life. You probably tend to have the most conflict with the people you trust the most. It's risky to engage in debate, but if you know the other person truly has your best interest at heart, you'll take the challenge. For me, the person I have the most conflict with is my wife, Lisa. She can tell me the hardest truth. Sometimes it hurts, but she has that freedom. I know she is looking out for my best interest.

The ability to increase trust is a key coaching skill. Unfortunately, it's rarely taught in management courses. It's the hidden factor that turns a good leader into a great leader. You can make a lot of mistakes in your leadership, but if your team trusts you, they will stay with you.

Building trust puts currency in your pocket. When you increase the trust, you get more coins. When you make a poor decision, you lose some of your trust change. The goal is to never have empty pockets. If you have empty pockets, you've lost your leadership.

When I first begin working with an organization, I always look for the real leader. Sometimes it's not the CEO or administrator of a company. At times, it's someone on the front lines or middle management. Contrary to some beliefs, leadership is not just a title. John Maxwell, author of *The 21 Irrefutable Laws of Leadership,* says, "Leadership is influence." The one with the greatest influence is the real leader. **Increasing influence requires trust.** People will not listen to you until they believe you have their best interest at heart.

When you look at it this way, leadership is a gift people give you. Leadership is a gift you must steward. It's not a right you can demand. You can't demand people to follow you. The best way

24

to determine who the real leader is, is to see who has the most followers.

Gaining trust quickly requires transparency. The more transparent something is, the easier it is to see through it. When you allow people to see into your heart and soul, they will have greater trust in you as the leader. Intimacy is the art of allowing people to see into you. I have the greatest intimacy with my wife because I allow her to see into my heart. She knows my goals, passions and struggles. The process of allowing her to continually see inside continues to build a trusting relationship where she doesn't misread my intentions — even when I say something I shouldn't!

Intimacy can be a scary proposition for many leaders. Questions they may ask themselves include: "Will people use the information against me?" "Will they back stab me?" It could happen, but I've discovered the value of "low-drama, high-results" is worth the risk.

There is an art to this. Don't walk into your team tomorrow and share all your dark secrets. I suggest you simply start with adopting a new phrase at the end of your directives. Begin by sharing your "why," not just the "what" or "how." **Using the phrase, "...and this is why..."** at the end of statements helps people understand your motives. They might not like the how or what of your system; but, if your team understands the why, they will give you their time and talents to help accomplish the goal.

Reflection & Action

To produce faster results, your job is to continually pump more trust into your team.

The greater the capacity to trust, the greater the capacity to execute.

Trust is like oxygen. You can't see it, but you know it when it's not there.

1. Is there anything, big or small, that is keeping you from trusting your people more than you already do?

2. BONUS: text DRAMAFREE to 864-901-7315 Ask Dennis to send you the massive trust building exercise for you and your team called Mad, Glad, Sad/Stop, Start, Continue; and the TSP Method. Or email dennis@leadershipprocess. com

Chapter 5
The 4 Drivers of Motivation

"People always behave in order to get a need met."

"People do not do things to hurt you. They simply act in a way to get their needs met," I explained to Kent as he tried to navigate his way through the disappointment in his executive team. His hospital was in a turnaround situation, and he had to release his CFO and COO for poor behavior. They had been with him a long time, but they were unwilling to change how they treated people. Though they were incredibly knowledgeable and skillful, their behavior was getting in the way of those talents. **Sadly, we may hire people for what they know, but we end up releasing them for who they are.**

At times, I'm part of the onboarding process at the executive level. One of the key questions I'm trying to discern is not, "Does this person have the skills to do the job?" If I'm looking at their resume and they are sitting in front of me, that's a forgone conclusion. The real question is, "Can this person succeed in this culture?"

An organization's culture is their collective beliefs and values. It's how they think and believe as a group. You see culture is how an organization behaves. Their actions are a reflection of their culture. An organization's behavior always follows its beliefs. I ask myself, "Does this person carry the same beliefs as the rest of the team?" You see their culture in the words they use.

Language is a reflection of culture. I spent over a decade living in Eastern Europe. When I first moved to Germany, I didn't know the German language. It took me months of agonizing study to come to a level of proficiency. There were so many rules in the language but no deviation. What I discovered is that is also the German culture. There are many rules and you've got to follow them.

Two years later we moved to Poland and began the process of learning another language. As we learned Polish, I saw there were even more rules than German. The difference was, there were many exceptions to every rule. This is a reflection of the Polish people. They're always creative and find a way around a rule. When I interview potential candidates I ask myself, **"Does this person have the same language as this team?"**

When you are clear on the culture you produce, hiring and firing becomes much easier. You'll notice people will begin to behave their way in and out of an organization. It doesn't become so personal. The key question becomes, "Can this person fit into our culture?"

There's a security people feel when values are clearly defined. They know they might make mistakes, but as long as they live and work with the company's values, they'll always have a spot on the team. And when people feel safe, productivity soars. **Challenges with people usually boil down to two conflicts: expectations or values conflict.** Becoming clear on both is the work of leadership.

Working to clarify values and expectations is real work. Because God has created each person uniquely, they have a certain lens through which they define expectations and values. They have a distinct way they are motivated.

These motivations are categorized into "four lenses." Understanding these four lenses helps you discover what's driving that person. If you're oblivious to these drivers, you'll end up trying to motivate people the way you're motivated. This only produces results with people who are like you. And because different people bring different talents to help your organization succeed, you need a mixture of talents to be successful.

Some leaders work to build a team of people that are exactly like them. Many times, this produces a dysfunctional team.

Not only do people behave according to their needs, they can also become overly dramatic if they can't meet their needs in a healthy way. **Many times, drama behavior is a tragic expression of an unmet need.** Helping people meet their needs in a healthy way is the best process to keep them out of drama. You can't meet someone's core need, but you can coach them through the process.

The Four Drivers of Behavior and the Constraints That Send Them into Drama

1. Forward and Direct

Some of your team are straight-forward and direct. If they have an opinion, you are going to know it. They don't hold back. These team members want to be in charge of something, even if it's just the coffee pot. They want to do and be something great. They're driven and decisive.

Give these people areas of clear responsibility, where they have the freedom to control the events liberating for them. When they don't get this need met in a healthy way they may try to control or manipulate people. They might become dictatorial and autocratic in their decision making.

2. Respect and Recognition

Others are completely opposite. They value respect and recognition. They want to connect on a personal level in order to feel a part of the team. They are specialists that typically like to see projects through to completion. They are motivated by stable environments.

An over extended need for approval can make this person go overboard trying to please everyone. They might not be as direct as they need to be because they are afraid of other's reactions. Not having a process for navigating changing environments can cause them to go into victim thinking and hinder results.

3. **Change and Variety**

You probably have others on your team that love change and variety. They have multiple projects and love a fast-paced environment. They love to connect with new people and influence others.

Don't box these people in with detail work. They need the freedom to create new possibilities. Just as with any gift, if you over extend it, that talent becomes a constraint. They tend to get bored easily and don't follow through as well as others.

They are not trying to frustrate you by bouncing from one project to the next. They simply have a need for variety, that if not met in a healthy way, becomes a detriment.

4. **Details and Accuracy**

Certainty is a driver that some possess. These people love the details and value accuracy. They are willing to do the research needed to ensure success. This strength over-extended can cause them to slow projects down. Their fear of being wrong stops them from moving forward. If the need for certainty isn't met in a heathy way, they can become critical or perfectionistic.

Understanding people's core drivers helps you have clear expectations of others. In different situations, we can embody each of these motives. Meaning is never found in just words, but in people. They can use the same words, but because of different motivations, the meaning changes for each person. When you clarify drivers, you actually clarify meaning. When people truly understand the meaning of their team members, team performance improves.

People do not do things to hurt you, they simply do things to get their needs met. I'm not saying their actions or words don't hurt. Many are so consumed with their needs that they become blind to their behaviors.

While I cannot control someone's actions towards me, I can control my response to their actions. In order to help me stay out of drama and to keep me proactive in my response, I ask myself: **"What need are they trying to meet?"** This question helps take the drama out of my response.

Understanding core drivers allows you to formulate a healthy response instead of a reaction. When you react negatively you always do more damage than good. Practically everyone has responded defensively to a situation and ended up making an adverse event even worse.

One of the best ways to help people stay out of drama is to show up healthy. Don't engage in their drama. Ask yourself: *"What is the need they are trying to meet?"* It helps you deal with them proactively instead of reactively.

Reflection & Action

The key question becomes, "Can this person succeed in our culture?"

1. List names or initials of individuals who come to mind when you think of each behavior style.

Forward & Direct

_____

_____

_____

Respect & Recognition

_____

_____

_____

Change & Variety

_____

_____

_____

Details & Accuracy

_____

_____

_____

2. Now, next to each name above, write down one or two specific things you could do to honor the other person's style.

Chapter 6
What's Driving Your Team?

"Motivation flows out of motive."

"Dad, you'll never believe it. 'Squared Eye' lives in Greenville." This was the statement Andrew, our oldest son hit me with as I walked through the door. After a five-day speaking tour in the Northeast I was tired and desperately wanted a day off. Truthfully, I didn't know what a 'Squared Eye' was, nor, did I care at the time.

Andrew explained, "'Squared Eye' is his Twitter name. He is a guy that I've been following on Twitter that I desperately want to meet. I just found out he lives in Greenville." Twitter is a social media site. I stored this conversation away in my memory and didn't think much of it. I was tired, hungry and ready for a break.

About a month later, I was enjoying a cup of Starbucks with a pastor friend of mine in our local area. He mentioned, "Dennis, there is a young family coming to my church. He's a successful designer that goes by the Twitter name 'Squared Eye'." It obviously piqued my attention.

Through a series of emails and calls, I arranged for Andrew and me to have breakfast with this world famous designer that happened to live in our home town. That meeting changed the trajectory of my son's life. It was a relationship that catapulted his career.

At the time, Andrew was set to attend Maryland Institute College of Art. After 60 minutes with Squared Eye, those plans changed. He explained to Andrew that with his skill set, there was a better path for him. He opened an opportunity for my son to intern with a technology incubator.

This resulted in Andrew starting his own business doing interface design. Today, Andrew is blessed with an amazing business doing the work he loves and making more money than most people do in their fifties. I remind Andrew to this day, **"What you do flows from who you know."** It's a lesson he'll never forget.

Bradley Cox was the pastor that connected us to Squared Eye (i.e. Matthew Smith). I'm forever grateful to him. In fact, I've done multiple projects at an incredibly reduced rate on multiple occasions for Bradley. Anything I can do for Bradley, I will. He blessed me in an arena that was very important to me. There is nothing I wouldn't do for him. He's a person that embodies the G.P.S. framework.

What is the G.P.S. framework? G.P.S. is a personal guidance system. It is likened to the GPS navigation system in a car. It stands for Goals, Passions and Struggles. I'll give more details on this later.

Think about the navigation system in your car. Most likely, if you own a newer model automobile, your vehicle possesses a navigational system.

You program it with your destination and it builds a roadmap allowing you to arrive at your destination. Your GPS tells you where to turn, which route to follow and what to avoid.

Each team member also possesses an internal G.P.S that's guiding their life. They might not be able to articulate it, but I guarantee you, they have a G.P.S. As a leader, you play the role of a detective. A person's navigation system is in there, and you must search it out. If you can find someone's G.P.S. you have the secrets to motivating them.

To play the role of a detective takes the skill of stepping outside of yourself. This is a major reason leaders don't see success. They can't see beyond their own needs, desires and goals to objectively look at their team. It's a subtle trap I don't want you to fall into. Don't become so focused on your desires that you lose sight of the fact that your team members also have goals. **The ability to step outside of yourself is the trademark of a great coach.**

In my workshops, I teach the "Golden Rule." I often ask people what they think of when I say the "Golden Rule." Most quote the famous passage, "Do unto others as you would have them do unto you." I completely believe in this rule. In fact, it's a quote from my all-time favorite leader. There wasn't a better leader than him. But this is not the rule I'm referring to. Others say, "He who has the gold rules." There might be some truth to this rule, but I think there is a higher principle.

The best leaders embrace and live out this higher "Golden Rule." It is, "There is gold inside of everyone."

Think about miners. Miners are people searching for gold. I think it takes a certain mindset to be a successful miner. When they enter the mine, they are not focused on the dirt. Their minds are laser pointed, looking for the gold. In fact, they become overjoyed with just the tiniest glimmer of gold. They don't focus on the dirt and all the work entailed in getting the gold out of the earth. **They are consumed with the gold. They ignore the dirt.**

Miners understand they most likely will have to move tons and tons of dirt to find just the most minute bit of gold, but they do it anyway. They labor and toil for mere ounces of that special yellow dust. Coaching people follows the same principle. You might have to move tons and tons of dirt in people's lives, but there is gold there. Great leaders are on a search for gold. They are convinced they will find the gold somewhere, and instead of focusing on the dirt they will have to sift through, **they focus on the gold**.

The best leaders operate the same way. They focus on the gold in people. They are not consumed with the dirt. **They don't look for what's wrong, but focus on what's right. "Where is the gold and how can I get it out of that dirt?"** is their key question. This mindset changes how they lead their team. I've learned that almost anyone can tell me what's wrong, but few have the ability to look at someone and tell me what's right.

You find whatever you focus on. If you focus on the dirt, I assure you, you will find it. But if you concentrate on the gold, it will appear. "I'm looking for gold," is the mantra of the drama-free, high-performance leader. Make it your mantra and notice what you discover. Using the G.P.S. framework helps you stay in the "looking for gold" mindset. There are three things motivating people. If you can discover them and tie your goals together, the synergy is amazing. It's the hidden secret to tremendous results.

It goes back to the **G.P.S. framework**. Do you remember? **It stands for Goals, Passions and Struggles.**

Everyone on your team has goals. There are certain outcomes they want to achieve. They possess dreams. Sometimes they might not even be aware of them, but I guarantee you, they are there. Your assignment as the leader of your team: Find those goals and figure out how you can help each person achieve those goals. If you help them get what they want, they in turn, will give you their hearts. Beautiful outcomes occur when you have your team's heart.

Each individual also has passions. They have desires. There are causes they are devoted to and different initiatives they are willing to give their lives for. Maybe it's breast cancer awareness or fly fishing. People are so unique, and each passion is unique.

You'll know if you've spent any time with me, I'm passionate about the Boston Red Sox, Apple computers and my kids. If you have a casual conversation with me, we'll probably come across those subjects. If you can find a way to assist someone in their passions, they will give you their heart. Just like when I asked Bradley Cox to help Andrew. I will do anything for Bradley now, because he helped my son. He has won my heart.

Lastly, there are struggles each person faces. No matter how successful a person becomes, there are constraints that hold them back from that elusive next level. I've seen that if I help someone overcome a challenge, I've gained their trust. I've won their heart and they love giving me their hand.

If you're having trouble getting someone's hand — that is, getting them to change their behavior — more than likely, it's because you haven't won their heart. **Win the heart, and the hand is the benefit.** If you focus on the hand, without the heart, people feel manipulated and abused. That's a terrible way to lead and one of the top reasons leaders have drama-filled teams.

Think about the people you are most grateful for in your life. Are there people that you would do anything you could to help them? It's probably because in some way they found part of your G.P.S. and assisted you in one of those arenas.

You can do the same for your team, as Bradley Cox did for me. When you help people with their G.P.S. you'll discover, there's nothing they won't do for you.

Reflection & Action

"What you do flows from who you know."

The ability to step outside of yourself is the trademark of a great coach.

The best leaders focus on the gold in people. They are not consumed with the dirt. They don't look for what's wrong, but focus on what's right.

"Where is the gold and how can I get it out of that dirt?" is their key question.

Everyone has their own G.P.S. Navigation. Discover this about someone and you begin to understand what motivates and drives them.

1. Give yourself the gift of private time to think about your own G.P.S.

a. What are your Goals?

b. What are your Passions?

c. What are your Struggles?

Chapter 7

Stop Asking Why

"The right questions direct your team's focus."

It was two o'clock on a Friday afternoon and I was looking forward to a coaching session with Cindy. She's an administrator with whom I enjoyed working. She was proactive and always accepted a challenge, but that Friday, things changed. I picked up the phone and was barraged with her complaints.

"Dennis, why do my nurses always complain? It's all I hear from the time I walk into the facility until I go home. They complain, bicker, and backbite nonstop. I've had enough. It seems that's all they do. Why do they do this to me?"

I responded, "Cindy, **do you really want to know why? Or do you really just want them to stop this behavior?**" I heard silence on the other end of the line. She had never thought about this before. The truth, really, was she just wanted them to stop complaining. Honestly, she didn't really care why. They just needed to produce results as a team and the bickering was hindering their progress. **The wrong question always produces the wrong perspective.** And when your perspective isn't clear, your focus is fuzzy. When you focus on the wrong things, results diminish.

If you're working on yourself and trying to root out the cause of faulty belief patterns, "Why?" is a great question to begin this process. I encourage leaders to ask themselves "Why?" all the time. It helps you dig down to the root belief of the poor behavior that's producing insufficient results. But when you're working with your team be careful in how you utilize the question "Why?" Over utilizing the question, "Why?" can produce mistrust in people instead of trust. And you desperately need to develop trust when working with people.

"Mark, why did you do it this way?" Frank demanded.

"It's because I didn't get the information from Sue. If I would have gotten the email, I could have changed how we did this." Mark responded.

I watched this interaction between Mark and Frank. The conversation lasted another excruciating ten minutes where I watched Mark continue to become a victim by blaming other people. The more Frank hammered the question, "Why?" the deeper Mark defended his position. I watched as they burned precious work hours having a conversation that produced no results. The common reaction to the question "Why?" is for people to defend their position. If you're honest, many times you don't want the answer to "Why?", you just want the problem solved and that particular behavior never done again.

What happens to you when you get hit with the question, "Why?"? If you are honest, you probably become defensive. You begin to give reasons to defend why you did what you did. If you're leading a results-based culture, many times, it doesn't matter "why." There are better questions that produce better results.

Asking "Why?" all the time produces a low-trust, low-performance culture based on the fear of consequences, where team members act like children, need to be told what to do, and rely on you to solve all the problems. You'll end up feeling like you're running an adult day care. But if you're willing to take the challenge of creating a high-trust, high-performance culture where people own their behavior and produce amazing results, then it's time to change the questions.

Questions direct people's thinking. It's through questions that you help people change. People always move in the direction of their most dominant thought. If you want to change actions, you begin by shaping their thinking.

You don't do that by demanding them to change their thinking. It's not accomplished through a new policy. **You change thinking by the questions you ask.** The questions you ask direct thoughts, which change actions, which produce results. Your questions determine your results.

He who asks the questions, controls the conversation. Have you realized you can be in complete control of a conversation without doing a majority of the talking? When you ask questions and people respond, you control the flow of conversation. It's the most powerful coaching tool you possess. You control the type of conversation you have with your team, whether it's productive or unproductive, according to the types of questions you ask.

One mistake I see leaders continually make is to only give answers to their team, and never ask them questions. If all you ever have are answers for your people, they will always come to you with questions. This dynamic creates child to adult conversations, where you tell people what to do. Being the center for answers actually creates people who are dependent on you. Then when you leave for vacation, they wonder what to do. Don't fall into this trap.

The guiding principle here is: Questions go down, answers come up. You should become the Chief Question Asker, not the Chief Answer Giver. Coaching people is about helping them change mindsets so they change their behavior. Changing mindsets starts with changing the questions.

"Dennis, you don't understand, I'm the problem solver. If my people have a problem they bring it to me and I solve it. As the leader of this organization that's my responsibility." Jim was adamant that as CEO, he was the Chief Problem Solver. This had been his framework for over twenty years. Unfortunately, he couldn't see this mindset was hindering the growth of his organization.

Here's the constraint that occurs when you take this position of being the Chief Problem Solver.

If all you ever do is solve my problems, then all I will ever bring to you is problems. When this occurs you develop a co-dependent relationship with your team. You teach them to come to you and you will fix their issue. Taken to the extreme, your organization revolves around you.

You become the person hindering the growth of your organization. Instead of just announcing solutions to your team, train them to solve their own problems. To create problem solvers, here's a key question I teach leaders to use:

"What are you going to do about that problem you have?"

It's a big question. Especially for people who are used to having you solve all their problems. This question becomes a game changer for your organization if you learn how to use it correctly.

Here are some reasons why I love using this question:

First, it assumes I believe you're powerful enough to solve your own problems. If I step in to save the day, I see you as a victim. I take the position of having to rescue you and fix your issue. This is what creates most co-dependent relationships with teams. The leader assumes the responsibility for fixing the person, instead of giving them the power to create a solution.

Second, this question directs people out of the victim mentality. It puts the responsibility for solutions with the team member not the leader. The question keeps their problems, their problems.

If you're not careful, different team members will try to make their problems, your problems. Don't let this happen to you. Remember, as a leader your job is to grow and train your team to solve problems.

Learning better questions generates better results. It's the questions you use that unlock people's hearts and minds. It allows you to go beyond using policies and procedures to create compliance.

When you understand someone's heart, you easily get their hand. This is real leadership. But if you focus on just getting their hands without their heart, you'll never have long term success with your team. You'll have a revolving door of people entering and leaving your organization.

It's the questions you use that generate your results.

Reflection & Action

Do you really want to know why?
Or do you just want them to stop this behavior?

Learning better questions generates better results.

It's the questions you use that unlock people's hearts and minds.

"What are you going to do about that problem you have?"

1. Are you rescuing someone on your team? If yes, how's that working for you?

2. Make a list of who you need to meet with, to help redirect their focus on solutions, by asking them, "What are you going to do about that problem you have?"

BONUS: text DRAMAFREE to 864-901-7315 Ask Dennis for his great list of Coaching Questions. Learning to ask better questions will accelerate your progress toward results.

Chapter 8

You Teach What You Know, but Produce Who You Are

"To create a drama-free team, become a drama-free leader."

Leading a team is very similar to leading a family. Children become a reflection of their parents' leadership. This thought was driven home to me early this year when I spoke at a conference in Austin, Texas. Typically, after I present, there is a group of people who want to speak personally with me, but when I presented that January day in Austin no one wanted to talk with me.

Andrew, my oldest son, had made the trip with me and was in the back of the room near my product table. After my talk, I looked to the back of the room to see a swarm of people around Andrew. What people wanted to know from Andrew is, "Is this McIntee guy really for real?" **I can teach you what I know, but if you want to really know who I am, just look at my children. It will tell you a lot about who I am. You produce who you are.**

One of my favorite things to do when working with organizations is to walk the halls and talk to the front-line staff. While you're not responsible for people's behavior, their actions tell me the story of the team's leadership. These conversations give great insight into their leader. While you can teach great principles and create fantastic guidelines, if people don't see you act in line with those ideals, those policies are worthless.

People see you before they hear you. I'm sure you've heard the statement, "Actions speak louder than words." Actions are powerful in building high-trust, high-performance teams.

I grew up playing the game, "Follow the Leader." You've probably played this game once or twice. The leader performs an action, and everyone followed behind. Leadership means you're out front. People watch you and follow your actions. Unfortunately, the game some leaders prefer to play is, "Simon Says." They stand there and dictate commands. Simon says, "Clean your desk!" and they expect people to obey. All the while, their office is a mess.

Nothing makes a better impression on people than the ability to lead yourself. Honestly, it's hard to lead others when you have trouble leading yourself. People see you before they hear you. What kind of leader are people seeing when they look at your life? How do you handle your own emotions? How do you manage your time? It's hard to coach others in arenas where you also struggle.

A good self-evaluation question to ask is, "How do I show up?" Remember you're showing who you are and the leadership game we are playing is, "Follow the Leader" not "Simon Says."

One of God's natural laws states that you reproduce after your own kind. Orange fruit trees do not produce apples. I would never expect apples from an orange tree. That's foolish. But how often do we expect different behavior from our team than we do from ourselves? When you ask your team to do what you're unwilling to do yourself, it's like asking for apples in an orange grove. It's simply ridiculous.

Being is more powerful than doing. When I work with leaders in setting goals, I first focus on who they are becoming not what they are going to do. **If you can become a big person, you will do big things**, but the opposite is not always true. Just setting big goals does not ensure you'll accomplish them. It's important to set big goals. Unfortunately, many stop there and then wonder why they aren't successful. If you focus first on becoming a big person, big goals are not a problem. Big people do big things. The first question you need to answer is, "Who do I need to become?"

I'm sure the question rolling around in your mind right now is, "Dennis, how do I become a big leader? I have big goals. I'm just not sure how I can become a big leader." I've developed the **ARM**™ **Methodology** to help leaders become bigger in order to accomplish greater results. This is a 3-step process that involves Awareness, Responsibility and Motivation.

Awareness

The first step involves awareness. In working with thousands of leaders across the globe, I believe the greatest need of leaders is constructive feedback on their own behavior.

Feedback is the key to increasing awareness. Receiving feedback is a great friend. Many leaders don't see it as a friend; they view it as an enemy. What you believe determines how you act. If you perceive feedback as an enemy you'll treat it as such; and unfortunately, you won't receive the benefit that it's there for you. If you see feedback as an enemy, you'll defend and justify your behavior. You won't extract the benefit from the information. But if you perceive it as a friend, you'll benefit from the data. If you view feedback as a friend, you'll thank the one who introduced you. With this mindset you can extract benefit from the feedback.

Big leaders don't shoot the messenger. Even when it's not delivered in a positive format, there is probably a sliver of truth to the message. Extract the truth from the message, learn from it, change your behavior and move on. That's how a high trust, high performance leader deals with feedback. You can't change what you don't see.

We all have constraints that limit our effectiveness. There are some schools of thought that teach you just need to work on your strengths. Don't worry about what you do wrong, just focus on those strengths. Other camps believe you need to work on those weaknesses.

It's a common question I receive in my workshops. My answer is, work on both. I believe completely in developing your strengths and focusing on what makes you great. But it's also true there are certain constraints you must overcome to be successful. For example, you might be gifted at creating sales opportunities but not real passionate about the details. Continue to hone your ability to sell while also creating processes to ensure the details don't fall through the cracks. In 25 years of working with leaders, I have discovered it's the person with the fewest constraints that wins. Become proactive by working in both arenas, strengths and constraints. Obtain feedback in both arenas and put together a personal development plan. If you need a couple of ideas on how to accomplish this, email me at **info@leadershipprocess.com** and I'll be happy to send you the exercise.

Responsibility

When you become aware, you have a choice. You can justify why things are that way or you can create a plan to change. It's your choice. You are ridiculously in charge of your own behavior! You won't change in any arena in which you blame and play the victim. Blaming others for what's happening in your life justifies yourself and removes responsibility.

I went through the process of losing more than 75 pounds. It's a remarkable story that I like to share during my keynotes. The main reason for the change in my behavior was my acceptance of responsibility. The funny story is I always used to blame my wife for my weight. She's an amazing cook. She likes to cook, and I like to eat. It's a great combination.

We went through a time in our lives where we had three of our children each two years apart. It felt like we were always pregnant. We would eat together through the pregnancy, but then when she gave birth, it only took her a few weeks until she returned to her normal weight. I never returned. I felt like I never had the chance to have a baby! It wasn't fair. Change didn't occur until I looked in the mirror and realized I was fat. Not chubby, but really fat. I had an epiphany.

Honestly, I never ate a doughnut accidentally. I chose to eat it. My weight was a reflection of my choices. I took responsibility for my choices and I obtained a different result. The good news is, you can do it, too.

Where you are in life is a direct result of the choices you have made. You are in charge of your choices. No one else is. It's time to stop playing the victim. You can't grow in any arena that you've become the blamer in.

Realize your team is a reflection of you. The culture in your facility is a direct result of your leadership choices. Change your leadership actions and your culture will change. My weight changed when I began to make different choices. It won't happen overnight, but keep sowing the seeds of great leadership actions and watch for the fruit. It will appear.

When you take responsibility for any arena in your life, whether it's finances, health, an organization, your marriage or any other area you're thinking about, you become responsible. When you justify and give reasons, you're not able to respond.

Let's be honest. Many times, the reasons are not important. What's most important is that the outcome changes. To change the result, I must begin with my actions. Your leadership actions create a result. If you don't like the result, change the actions.

Winston Churchill once said, "The price of greatness is the acceptance of responsibility." Great leaders take responsibility for the culture of their organization. They know the buck stops here. They don't blame or complain. They put on their big boy or big girl pants and get to work. If you want a change in your organization, first, change yourself. You grow yourself first, then your team grows. Watch then, as your whole organization grows. Organizational growth flows from personal growth.

Motivation

Even though I've seen my blind spots and decided to take responsibility to change, it won't happen overnight. This is where sustaining motivation needs to kick in. Personal development demands more than a McDonald's® drive through approach. I like it fast and quick just like everyone else, but I have to tell you the truth. Change takes a process. You won't change overnight so please don't expect your team to change that quickly. Leadership is baked in a slow cooker not a microwave oven.

Focus is the key to motivation. How you focus determines how you feel. If you focus on the problems it won't take long for anger to rise. Once that occurs, you've lost your personal power. When you're angry, you're not creative or constructive. You can't help your team when you're mad at them. If you are, change your focus.

The power of your life is in the focus of your life. Think of a light. When it's diffused it will light a room, but if you focus it like a laser beam, that same light can cut through steel. The power of your life is in the focus of your life.

My friend Mike Murdock, singer-songwriter and pastor at The Wisdom Center in Texas, says, "The reason people fail is broken focus." You can trace any failure in your life to broken focus. As leaders, we need to guard our focus. Your life always moves in the direction you focus, and the greater the focus, the greater the results. If you're not producing the results for yourself personally, first examine your focus. This is the secret to great leaders. Your focus determines your personal direction. This, in turn, governs your organizational direction. If I want to change an organization, I first have to work to change the leader. When the leader changes, the team changes.

Grow yourself, grow your team, grow your organization. It works in that order. Don't mix it up. When YOU change, your team will begin to change.

You teach what you know, but produce who you are!

Reflection & Action

I can teach you what I know, but if you want to really know who I am, just look at my children. It will tell you a lot about who I am.

You produce who you are.

Being is more powerful than doing. If you can become a big person, you will do big things.

AWARENESS:

Feedback is your friend! If you can see it, you can change it!

Tell me what you did today, and I'll tell you who you are.   **—Mahatma Gandhi**

RESPONSIBILITY:

When you become aware, you have a choice. You can justify why things are that way or you can create a plan to change. It's your choice. You are ridiculously in charge of your own behavior!

Where you are in life is a direct result of the choices you have made. You are in charge of your choices. No one else is. It's time to stop playing the victim. You can't grow in any arena in which you've become the blamer.

MOTIVATION:

Focus is the key to motivation. How you focus determines how you feel. If you focus on the problems it won't take long for anger to rise. Once in which occurs, you've lost your personal power.

The power of your life is in the focus of your life.

NEXT STEPS

I've become frustrated at times when reading leadership books. I think, "How in the world can I accomplish what the author is espousing? He must be living in a different world." Let me assure you, I know exactly where you are. I'm sure there were times you were reading this book and thought, "That's a great philosophy but he doesn't know my team." I've been there.

The great question is, "What are you going to do next?" You won't change your team overnight. It's a fallacy to think otherwise. Over the course of many years, you've behaved yourself into the place you are. Just as you don't change overnight, don't expect your team to be different instantly. There's no magic bullet that's going to change your organization overnight.

What you can do is begin today. You can make changes in your leadership style that over time will alter your results.

Ask yourself, **"What's one thing I can do today to make a measurable difference in my team?"** Whatever that answer is, do it! That's my best advice for you. If you don't do something, don't expect different results. Truthfully, if you're unwilling to take action, no one, including me, can help you.

After you take action, monitor your results. If you're not happy with your results, change your actions. Actions are the one thing you are ridiculously in charge of. Your behavior determines your results.

You CAN create a drama-free team that creates BETTER results, with LESS STRESS, MORE TRUST & GREATER COURAGE!

Dennis

About the Author

"Dennis has helped changed the culture of my company" - this is the common phrase clients use to describe Dennis' work within organizations.

For the last 25 years, Dennis has traveled extensively working with leaders to uncover their personal and organizational constraints in order to build high-trust, high-performance cultures. The first 15 years of his career was in pastoral ministry in the U.S. and Europe.

A whole new world opened up to Dennis when he realized that these same principles that changed people's lives could also change their companies. In 2004, he formed **The Leadership Development Group** to help leaders win at the game of work and the business of life.

Dennis is passionate about helping leaders develop their coaching skills. When a leader improves, his organization improves. He keynotes frequently at leadership seminars, as well as, appearing in magazines, newspapers, trade journals, and on national radio and TV.

He is the author of *The Power of Pursuit*, *People Smart* and *Time Mastery*.

For more video and audio training, Dennis' Podcast, and the latest updates and research

breakthroughs in building and leading Drama
Free Teams:

www.DramaFreeBook.com
www.DennisMcIntee.com

How to Contact Dennis

If you are interested in learning how to develop your coaching skills to get more from your team, Dennis can help. For more information about keynotes, trainings, workshops and coaching, contact **The Leadership Development Group**:

Email: info@leadershipprocess.com
Online www.dennismcintee.com

To purchase bulk copies of this book at a discount for your organization, please contact **The Leadership Development Group:**

Email: **info@leadershipprocess.com**
Phone: 864-901-7315

If you have an upcoming event, with or without dates already reserved, and you would like to learn more about Mr. McIntee's keynote speaking, or his change management consulting, please contact his consulting business partner:

Steven Rowell   steven@stevenrowell.com
                   610-909-0792 (cell)

For your convenience, please feel free to reserve a time for a quick discovery call via:

www.talkwithsteven.com